Sara

or the existence

of fire

by Sara Woods

Cover illustration and title text by Aidan Koch.

Sara or the Existence of Fire was designed and typeset by
Sara Woods in Garamond Premier Pro, Gill Sans MT and
Goudy Bookletter 1911.

This book is published by Horse Less Press in Grand
Rapids, MI. www.horselesspress.com and is distributed by
SPD / Small Press Distribution, Inc. www.spdbooks.org.

Table of contents

For all Saras

"..oh each poet's a beautiful human girl who must die."

-Alice Notley, *World's Bliss*

"Sara, you are the poet in my heart."

-Stevie Nicks, *Sara*

THERE was a family who lived in a small cottage on a beach somewhere. They had a little girl named Sara. Sara used to spend her days finding shells. She loved swimming down and touching sand under the water, letting it run through her fingers. She became an expert in black, soggy, half-buried things that you could only tell apart by smelling. Her mother was made of moths, and Sara used to go to sleep with a light by her bed so her mother would gather near her while she slept, their warm dog lying across her legs.

Sara used to lie still on her back in the waves by her parents' house. She would let them take her wherever they wanted to. She would just stare into the sky until she had arrived at the new home the waves had decided for her. It always ended up looking a lot like her old one.

Sara's father was a wolf.
Sara's mother was always
getting on his back about
his sheep-killing problem.
Her father said it's not a
problem and gosh. Sara was
always getting on his back
and riding through fields of
grass which was fun.

Sara's interview *with* *someone*

F: I don't know what you look like yet.
S: That's fine.
F: This is still being written, it may not be finished for years.
S: I know.
F: I'm a wolf for some reason.

When Sara sat down for breakfast this morning she felt like she was sitting on the bones of her family. She realized that while she was home for the holidays she had spent most of her time fantasizing that she was in a room full of pleasant strangers who kept giving her pie. Each year everyone is older and easier to ignore, which is a certain kind of vengeance. All of Sara's friends are learning to love their relatives and Sara is slowly killing her whole family with a flaming sword made of old age and natural causes. She wants to see their funerals and put them inside her body and feel the wounds of her grandfather's twenty-one gun salute.

pow pow pow pow pow pow pow
pow pow pow pow pow pow pow
pow pow pow pow pow pow pow

Sara's first pet was a giant fire. She used to feed it things she didn't want, things she found around the house. It ate the house and Sara's next pet was the foot of a hairy man. She would scratch it and kiss it all over. They were the best of friends. This was years ago.

Sara's parents died when she was young from a hunter and old age. Sara went to live with her aunt, who was a bear sound effect that emitted from tinny toy speakers. Sara did nearly what she wanted but never quite shook her aunt, who was always always in her, judging. A bit-crushed growl soundtracked her unpaid bills and slept-in mornings. Sara wrote a song about it:

aunt bear, aunt bear
back again with sara

When she was a girl Sara
liked to take baths. She
would lay with her ears
submerged and think about
tongues and knock on the
tub-floor and watch the
water change color when
she peed.

Sara's kitchen had a bookcase in it with a vase on top. The vase was filled with fake pink roses. The pink roses pointed at nothing in particular. There was a ceiling fan overhead that turned much too slowly to circulate air. The vase was made of red translucent plastic. The vase didn't know why it was there. None of us do.

Sara worked for a while at a place that made cookies. She would secretly touch the cookies all over when the owners and customers weren't looking. She told herself she did this to broadcast her particular set of microbes as widely as possible. Sara hated the idea that she might be someone that a person would have to get used to, even on a chemical level. Her boss knew about this, though he never let on. He secretly wanted to see Sara's germs spread widely through the city like a terrifying prayer. This is how he loved her.

Sara's dog is a miracle with four hairy legs that twitch when he is sleeping. She wants to taste his little claws sometimes, wants to use her teeth to get the black gunk out from underneath them just feeling the little nails sliding between her teeth across her lips one at a time carefully so she doesn't wake him up. She can feel the little pads on her lower lip scratchy but like good somehow. Her tongue wants to go find the webbed parts on these strange little inhuman feet. Sara wants to look at her dog and have their eyes meet and take all of his ear inside her mouth and whisper you are like the most beautiful salad.

Sara ate lunch usually at a place
down the street because the
waitress there would see her
and smile and say same thing?
and Sara would nod and say
same thing. Sara never touched
the fortune cookies because
once she opened one and it
said you are a brown brown leaf
and this is how dying feels.

Sara woke up with a dry mouth full of seeds. She sputtered and wheezed upon waking, spitting them onto her pillow. Sara's dog ate a few of the seeds. She took a handful and rinsed them in the sink. The water made them shine green in her hand. Sara took the seeds and planted them all over her apartment. Three or four she pushed down into the cracks in her couch cushions. Others she put in the pockets of old coats she hadn't worn in ages. Coats with broken zippers and missing buttons that she'd meant to get fixed before the winter was over. The winter had been over for some time now. She took eight seeds and placed them in old coffee mugs that were sitting around her apartment. Sara had not done dishes in ages, and these were plentiful throughout the house. She found other places for the seeds too: in the glass dome that covered the burnt-out ceiling light in her kitchen, in the speaker cracks of her television, inside an old dictionary and an old phone book, in her VCR that hadn't been used in years, in the dusty old owl bank that she'd had since she was a child. She put them everywhere she could think. She even swallowed a few, and they tasted like tiny salt pills going down. Over the next few weeks she watered them with nonsense whispers, told them her dream about climbing a telephone pole and seeing the whole city burn down around her. The sprouts came up then, green and shining, almost luminescent in her dimly-lit home. One sprouted out her ear, one out of her dog's back. Then came the pickles. They grew thick and plump, shining wet with brine. Her whole apartment began to reek of salt and dill. She picked an armful (nowhere near a peck), and placed them in white folding chairs in her kitchen. For company.

The dirt behind Sara's apartment was full of worms. They lived there, like Sara lived in her apartment. The worms weren't organized like ants. Sara was also not organized. On mornings when she was up, early early mornings after the worst nights, she would put her fingers down between the worm bodies. Index worm-part middle worm-part worm-part ring worm-part pinkie. The sun was not even up yet. Worm-part worm-part. The sun was after her.

Sara used to imagine her food as haunted by the ghosts of the individual ingredients. Bread was filled with wheat-ghost and yeast-ghost, salt-ghost and egg-ghost. Every bite she took she felt--or imagined she felt--these spirits of plants and minerals, animals and things-from-animals, sliding down past her teeth, deep into her. The ghosts would stay there, hang around and have conversations about Sara that she couldn't hear.

Did you see her hair today?

I know! A disaster!

You know, I don't think she even bathes anymore.

Sara met a mountain at a party. She didn't remember whose party it was, or why she had decided to come. It was someone's party. The mountain was holding a red solo cup and talking to a pretty girl. He told her he met Pete Sampras once. Pete was a really cool guy, the mountain said. The girl was very impressed. She said the tennis player right. The mountain didn't even justify this with a response. Sara wanted to scale him and stick a flag in his eye. The mountain was too big for the two-bedroom apartment they were in. Everyone was standing on his foothills but he didn't seem to notice or care. The party went really late. Sara met a woman who used to be in the circus there and she talked to her for a long time. She had wonderful stories. The party went so late that Sara and the few last stragglers got to see the sun rise over the mountain during their morning bus ride home. Sara had to admit it really was beautiful.

Sara went on a date with a large crowd of people. They had asked her out all in unison, so loud that two-thirds of them missed it when she said okay. They picked her up in so many cars that her entire street was filled, and it took her too long to figure out which one to get into. She could have gotten into any of them. They drove her to a fancy restaurant the size of a football stadium, and she sat at a table in the middle while her date surrounded her on all sides. She kept turning and trying to focus on one face or another, tried to recognize one or two. The crowd was made up of men and women of all ages. They roared small talk at her, and she would only catch a word here and there. She didn't have any answers, but this was okay because the large crowd of people was mostly looking at her eyes anyway. They all paid for her dinner, each of them contributing an eighth of a penny, and then she took a walk with them, because it was a nice night out. They all poured into the streets and backed up traffic for miles. Sara asked them where they all lived and how did they all meet and how did they keep from becoming a riot. At least half the crowd thought she was complimenting their sense of humor when she said this. After the walk Sara told the crowd she had had a nice time. The crowd tried to give her their phone numbers but Sara said maybe they could just call her instead. Sara received so many phone calls over the next few days that she changed her number. She had meant it when she said she'd had a nice time, though. She really had.

Sara always felt her limbs working. She would whisper hello to them all of the time and thank you and good job. Sara's limbs appreciated the encouragement. She used to cry at nights. Planet-sized sobs that would turn her back and legs in ways that backs and legs shouldn't turn.

This morning Sara found a bear in her shower. She got up to pee and was peeing, sitting quietly on the toilet when she noticed the sound of bear-breathing behind the shower curtain. She didn't run away or open the curtain, she just stared at it. For a long time. Maybe the bear was staring back at her. Staring at same spot on the other side of the curtain. Maybe she should get in and turn on the water. Maybe his fur would be nice and warm. Would he start killing her? Wouldn't he have started killing her now if he was going to kill her? Did he know she was there? Sara wanted to feel the pads on his paws with her fingers. The bear wanted to smell her hair. Sara finished peeing.

Sara found two more bears in her apartment. One was a cub that was curled up sleeping in her dog's bed. The other was its mother, which was attached by cables to the ceiling. She petted the cub's soft fur and saw the mother above, struggling against the cables. She put her hands on the cub's ears and said you don't have to hear anything you don't want to and I'm sorry for where you are right now, there should be trees here. The mother bear told her thank you for being so gentle with my cub but I will have to eat you when I get down. The trees that weren't there grew big and strong and then died and fell and new ones grew in their place. Sara used one of the fallen ones to create a canoe that wasn't there. She curled up in it and pretended she was a little girl again, fast asleep in bed. She imagined everything going in reverse until the bears weren't there anymore. She rewound it all until nothing was left but empty space and she was just another thing along with every other thing that wasn't there. No one was eaten.

Sara's dog decided he didn't like coffee. He sniffed at it for a few minutes before he actually tried it, and the smell seemed nice, maybe a little bitter, but with some milky sweetness. The taste wasn't at all appealing, though. He had found the coffee in a puddle that had collected from the tipped-over mug that was on the bathroom floor. Sara had been holding the cup for most of the morning while she was lying there, even for awhile after she stopped moving. When her fingers finally stiffened, the cup tilted just a little too far and the coffee-puddle grew out around her quickly, like a cloud of smoke. Coffee, he decided, was not for him.

Sara's dog wanted to
sleep in a giant salad.
He wanted to have a
tomato as a pillow,
and nothing would
ever wake him up.

Sara used to push almonds into her mattress so they would be watered with sweat at night. The almonds took root and grew into plants. There was a morning when Sara woke up in a salt garden without anything on. She dried the leaves like herbs and mixed them with tobacco for smoking. These are not drugs she told her dog. This is from almonds.

Sara woke up this morning with tattoos she hadn't seen before. They were drawn small and careful across her chest, three symbols she didn't know. She touched them and they were smooth and old like they had been there longer than she had. Sara's dog came over to say hi and she said do you know what these are? but he didn't know. The tattoos stayed. They weren't dream-tattoos, just tattoos and Sara didn't know how to find their meaning. She hid them at first but then became more open about wearing things that let parts of the symbols peek out. They made her more adventurous. She began to be a more courageous person because of the tattoos. She sometimes wondered if the symbols meant something like that, like courage.

Sara was at her cousin's house. Sara's knees were holding a soda, and there was a plate balanced on her thighs. Sara's cousin had invited Sara over to sit in a chair while she talked on the phone to her boyfriend. Or at least this is what ended up happening. The boyfriend, as far as Sara could tell, was a cockroach. Her cousin kept talking about the spines on his legs. At one point the cousin was talking about how she wished the boyfriend would be more independent, do things with just her and not always with his family. She paused and said she knew they used emergence behavior to eat but maybe she could bring back some rotting meat for everybody after they had some alone time. Sara sipped her soda. It didn't seem like things were going well for her cousin. Sara wanted to comfort her, but was afraid she would drop her food if she got up. The cousin said it's okay and I love you and I'll see you soon and okay and bye and hung up the phone. Sara asked her how work was going.

Sara found a cockroach on
the floor in her bathroom.
She scooped it up in her
hands and held it to her ear.
Lo siento it whispered.

Sara's dog's interview
with the
cockroach

D: I am smelling you and I do not know what you are.

C: ...

D: There are sticks in the yard that smell like you but not quite.

C: ...

D: You could be a thing to eat like berries.

C: ...

D: I am always eating berries.

The author's interview
with the
cockroach

A: When I was little I used to think about going to outer space.

C: You wanted to be an astronaut?

A: Yes. Or just to go up there.

C: You'd need a space suit, though.

A: That's true.

A giant fire's interiew with Sara's house

F: I'm sorry if I'm bringing you down.
H: That isn't funny.
F: I know.
F: I'm sorry.

Sara took a picture of her and me from the wall and broke it on the kitchen floor. She took part of the wood frame and lit it and made it into a torch. She took the torch and began lighting all of our things on fire. Our desk on fire. Our towels on fire. Our bed on fire. Our rug on fire. Our clothes on fire. Our tv on fire. Our cabinet on fire. Our books on fire. Our chairs on fire. Our table on fire. Our notebooks on fire. Our food on fire. She turned on the gas and set our stove on fire. The torch burned down close to her hand and so she threw it onto the floor and left the apartment. She went outside and got on a bus that went to a train that went to a beach. There were lights, it was night. The lights reminded her of the fires and she closed her eyes and tried to make them go away. She tried to make the fires go away because she didn't want any more fires then. She made a pile of sand and hugged the pile of sand to her, but her arms went through it. She laid down and tried to dig holes to put her arms in so she could hug the beach that way but she couldn't get the holes deep enough for her arms to go in without the sides of the hole collapsing. The sand was too dry and she wasn't crying enough. Sara walked into the water and it was too cold but she kept walking into it. She laid down in it face first and kicked the water as hard as she could. She kicked the water pretty hard. She thought about the torch and the apartment and before and then she stopped thinking about it. Sara wanted to feel wanted. She thought maybe she was wanted now, for arson. Sara was soggy and sandy and so she stood up out of the water and got on another train that went to another bus somewhere.

Sara's house caught on fire and she had to move to another house. That house caught on fire and she had to move to another house. That house caught on fire and she had to move to another house. When that house caught on fire Sara moved to 1000 houses, which was surprisingly affordable. All of the houses caught on fire and Sara moved to a beach, which was already on fire. Sara looked out at the sea and said this is my life. She said I am here for moving and fire. Sara's dog liked the beach because of the smells. Smells are secret messages from the universe to dogs on which we occasionally get to eavesdrop.

Sara wanted to marry a beach
somewhere with little trees
that don't have enough branches.

She wanted to	heavy
lay in the	rain
ocean salt	sits
with not	down
enough to	cloud
eat.	cloud

Everything would be on fire on
this beach cloud the ocean cloud
on fire cloud the skinny trees
cloud cloud on fire cloud.

Sara would marry	the beach
cloud in an	orange setting
could sky like	an overfilled
knife wound	cloud
cloud.	Cloud

don't cover us! Rain,
don't rain on our wedding.
All the guests are cloud
so happy and excited
cloud for our engagement.

Sara's apartment roof was a funeral home. Every night she went to sleep to shuffling mourners' feet and muffled condolences. On nights she felt brave she would put on all black and climb the fire escape. She would spend the evening sneaking potato salad and filling styrofoam cups with folgers decaf. The funeral home was on a roof and so it had no roof and so the murmurs of the mourners would bleed out and up, to the street and to space. She would bring her dog and he would stand and nobly let the little black-suited wake-boys touch his ears and neck and say good dog good dog good dog good dog. On those nights the rooftop mirrored the sky. The casket was the looming moon and Sara and the wake-people were all their own stars. Sara's dog was a distant galaxy, seemingly smaller than everything else around him, but with the quiet confidence of a body that knows it contains trillions.

Sara's apartment kept getting flies in it. The flies got in her food and in her drinks. They got in her refrigerator and in her dog's food. The flies were small, like fruit flies. At least at first. Then small flies began pouring through the windows in numbers like she's never seen before and larger, fist-sized flies began accompanying them. The little flies began to coat every imaginable surface. The flies got in Sara's nose and in her mouth. She could feel them coating the insides of her. Sara couldn't move in her apartment without feeling fly bodies pressing on her from all sides. The flies were everywhere. Her dog suffocated after one of the large flies muscled its way into his mouth. Sara tried to come to him, to save him, but she couldn't move because there were flies pushing against her from all sides. She couldn't even see his body after he died because of the flies on her eyeballs, pushing up under the insides of her eyelids. Sara tried to leave, tried to move, tried to do anything at all and realized she couldn't. The flies were too numerous, and had gotten into too many places. The sheer mass of the flies' swarm kept her from even falling to the ground. She gave up and let herself hang there, upright and limp in what used to be her kitchen but now was just flies.

Sara had a wreath on her front door until one day it disappeared. She replaced the wreath and again, it disappeared. The same thing happened the next day, and the one after that. This happened every day for 100 years. Sara lived and lived but felt like she was dying with the loss of each wreath. 1000 years passed, then 5000. Sara never seemed to get used to losing the wreaths, but became very comfortable with the idea of dying. After 10000 years Sara, now old beyond all comprehension, burned down her house and laid in a river. The river was older than she was, but not by much. She let herself drift down it, the whole time thinking of wreaths. She was so, so tired.

Sara nightmared that her childhood bedroom was entirely made of hair just four walls of human hair and her mom was mad and kept telling her to cut the hair cut the hair Sara cut the hair. When she woke up it felt like everything was exploding and there was no one there had someone been there had someone? Sara's dog was there. She stared at him and made a face until he licked it. To Sara's dog, their apartment was a great country and licking was his civic duty. He was a soldier. A patriot.

Sara's interview
with her
dream

S: My dog has learned how long it takes me to smoke a cigarette.

S: Every day I take him outside, let him out in the backyard, light a cigarette. He runs out into the yard, sniffs around, pees, poops.

S: He comes back and waits by the door just as I am finishing it. He's a smart dog.

D: I think you might be giving him too much credit. Dogs are good at learning routines.

Sara's dog spent most of his time in yards. Yards are rectangles of grass that people send you out to pee in.

Sara had to leave her apartment because of a problem. She scooped her dog into her arms and said oh baby oh baby my puppy puppy puppy we are going to a friend's because our home is dark and cold. Sara's dog gave her a look that was billions of years old and made her think of grapes.

Sara had an ocean inside her ears that wouldn't go away. She went about her day as usual, but she was always there, treading, scanning the 360° horizon for any sign of beach. She felt waves as she rode the bus. She felt the cold on her feet and the heat on her scalp as she locked her door. She felt her limbs losing strength as she let her dog outside. It was killing her.

Sara's interview with the author

A: I am giving you paws. Do you want paws?
S: I don't want paws.
A: I am giving you paws. You'll like paws.

Sara loved touching the snow. She liked how it emphasized the size and distance of the air, the space around her. Her dog would leave tracks like pairs of semi-colons, making a crooked line across her back yard.

;;
;;
;;
;;
;;
;;
;;
;;
;;
;;
;;

Sara's dog did not care what his tracks looked like. That is a thing humans think about but dogs don't. To Sara's dog the snow smelled like a thing that could kill him if he gave it the chance. He would not give it the chance.

The author's interview
with Sara

A: What were you doing?

S: I was staring at the ceiling, staring at the light hanging above the toilet.

A: Then?

S: I was letting the dog out because he couldn't sleep and then I couldn't sleep.

S: I was trying not to wake you up and you told me there was all this tungsten.

S: I was trying to remember what tungsten was. I knew it was on the periodic table.

S: Maybe it is a metal? I don't remember.

S: I was trying just to get back in bed and to go to sleep even though I knew I couldn't sleep.

S: I was smoking a cigarette, getting one last one in before bed.

S: I was looking at people on the internet while you were asleep in our bed.

S: I was drinking the last of the lemonade.

S: The last of the lemonade I brought home from work.

S: I talk about work so much now.

A: It's okay.

S: I was not crying. I was trying to cry.

A: Did you fall asleep?

S: I was building these weird heavens for us for later.

A: Is this a dream?

S: They kept collapsing. Everyone looked like bear people.

A: I can't tell if you're listening to me.

S: The bear people were okay. I meant the bear people.

S: It was the collapsing, it kept happening and I couldn't stop it.

A: What were you doing then?

S: I kept trying to start over, to make it work but I kept getting caught in these same same cycles.

A: That sounds frustrating.

S: It was.

S: Then I was waking up, realizing about dreams. That those were dreams before.

A: With the bear people? And the heavens?

S: There was all this tungsten.

A: And then what?

S: Trying to get back to that dream, the collapsing and bear people one.

A: Why?

S: I could fix it now, I knew I could somehow.

Sara went to sleep next to her dog and when she woke up she was in a new, vast bed. She spent years traveling the bed searching for the dog but only ever found signs of him, some of which were very, very old. I may never find him she said. I can only wait for him to return to me in this lonely place.

Sara talked to a placeless woman about the end of sadness. It's coming said the woman. Sara pointed out that she was on fire and the woman mostly said screams after that. Sara knew they would spend the rest of their lives together.

Sara took the woman into her car and they
travelled and as they travelled they took turns
coughing like it was a conversation. The
showers of strangers seemed to spite them,
saying you don't belong here what are you
doing what are you doing in me get out get
out.

No one asked them what they meant when
they said terrifying new things and Sara
found ways of twisting her hair up that made
her look like she knew what she was doing.
They would pull into towns like elephants
and the placeless woman would ask locals to
donate to their fund and by the way did they
want know how sharp knives are? because she
could show them it would be no trouble no
trouble at all.

Sara was in a room full of hammers. There were probably 10000 hammers in this room. Sara was shin-deep in hammers. There were no shelves or drawers or hooks, nowhere to put the hammers. Sara shuffled her feet and moved around the room, pushing the hammers out of the way. She wasn't sure what she was looking for. A trap door or something. Sara didn't find any trap door, after spending a long time moving her feet around, through the hammers. She picked a couple up and threw them around, just because. She took a big one and used the hammer to hammer on the other hammers. She laid down on top of the hammers like it was a hammer-beach made of hammer-sand. The ceiling was white and Sara told it hello. That was the first time anyone had ever talked to that particular ceiling. Sara thought about her childhood and her parents. About her dog. Where was her dog?

Sara felt the first of some
rain coming down on her as
she walked home. A drop. A
pause. A drop. A pause. A
pause. A pause. A drop. She
felt there was a rhythm to it.
Like morse code, but not. It
was telling her her life was
wrong.

Sara woke up with a fever in her that was pushing hard on her skin from the inside, making it red and hot. The clock by her bed held a three and two perfect zeroes. The fever made it unbearable for any part of her to touch any other part of her and so she went outside and lay all spread out in the cool grass. The whole world had shrunk down with fog and was sitting around her house. The moon had gotten lost at some point in all of this. Sara was worried about the moon. A forest she had never seen before grew gently up next to her and her dog ran away into it. Sara used her fever against the cold air and pressed her way into the forest to find him.

After a short time in the forest Sara no longer remembered her dog's name, and began trying out different names she thought she might have had for him. Henry! she called. Will-o-the-wisp! Bug-mover! Gravy needs!

The dog seemed to be nowhere. Sara was also nowhere by this point, but it was a different nowhere and she and her dog sat down, fog-caged in their respective nowheres. Their mouths said help us to the moon. From a third nowhere the moon said I am sorry, it turns out I am in a similar situation.

Sara's dog was falling. He felt wind whipping up past his fur, pushing his ears around. There is a placelessness to falling, if it's far enough. It doesn't matter much where you're falling to. Sara's dog spent his time falling understanding how you can move a body when there's no ground under you. How fast you can spin. How hard it is to stop spinning once you start. Sara's dog forgot where he was falling from. He never knew where he was falling to. He never really found out.

Sara's dog found cat-bodies everywhere he went. He tried to step over them but there were too many. His paws sunk and he stumbled trying to walk over them all. Some of them were alive. Some of them he couldn't tell. Where did all these cat-bodies come from.

Sara's dog couldn't sleep at night. He would wake up and find he had coughed up fourteen wasps. They were all dead. Where did these wasps come from? he asked himself. I didn't eat any wasps.

Sara's dog noticed his legs. He noticed his fur and his ears and his snout. Sara's dog noticed the sky. The sky appreciated this about him, and always looked at him lovingly. Sara's dog made footprints with his feet sometimes, made sounds with his throat. Some of the sounds he made were heartbroken. A dog can be heartbroken.

Sara's dog spent four years living in a cloud that was on fire. He rented it for cheap, because it was on fire. The landlord was a terrible, boring jazz band and Sara's dog paid rent by making himself vomit monthly in the landlord's trumpet. The cloud was a small, dirty one and Sara's dog did experiments to try and make himself glow bright enough to be seen through the cloud and the fire when he was at home. He never knew how well they turned out because he didn't have a friend to watch from outside and report back. I always wanted to tell him how beautifully he glowed.

Sara wrote a poem about dying. In it
Sara was an old woman and Sara was
a baby and no one took care of the
old woman and no one took care of
the baby. Sara wrote all the letters of
the poem down and squinted at
them like a cat nearly asleep. She
showed it to a man and the man
coughed out loud and said he used
to be a baby too. Everything Sara
had ever written was a prelude to
something she hadn't written yet.

Sara wrote a play. In it, two people
are standing in a room and each of
them is a beautiful beach. The sun is
setting over one of the beaches. The
two people are looking at each other,
and speak to each other in wave
crashes and seagull caws. Their tides
move in sympathy with one another.

the first one pulls   *the second pushes*

       the second pushes   *the first pulls*

they give   *each other*

       salt-wind   *as gifts.*

beach glass   *beach glass*

       the room fades away.   *they actually*

are   *beaches.*

       beach glass   *beach glass*

beach glass   *beach glass*

The one with the setting sun
whispers something to the one with
the sun overhead. She says
sometimes we have to let go.

In the afternoons, Sara would sit on the beach and watch her dog bite waves. She looked at the sky and the clouds up in it. Nothing had ever seemed so beautiful to her as this. She came up with a word for the feeling. She called it sandhaven. Sara wrote a short story on the beach one day about sandhaven.

SANDHAVEN

by Sara

In those days there was a feeling that everything could fall apart at any minute. The sky was black more often than it had ever been before. We were also horses those days. Horses weren't the strangest things we had been. The people of our village at different times had the bodies of starfish, of gigantic winged creatures with strange, electric fur, of tiny men with hands shaped like rose-thorns, of things made of fire and sound that are impossible to describe, let alone learn how to live in the bodies of. But each of those things, while strange and difficult at times, never lasted. These horse-bodies, they hung on too long. More than the dark sky or the thick air that settled in, I think it was these bodies that had everyone feeling nervous. Were we just horses now? Forever?

It wasn't a bad thing to be, honestly. Marcus and I made the best of it. Today we were out together, just us. Usually we didn't leave the village except in packs, but the rules seemed to be slipping as everyone's grip on reality was strained. Marcus and I felt it too, but it seemed to manifest in us something different, less like doom and more like recklessness. The horse-bodies felt strong and we were driven to find their limits.

As we ran along the beach a feeling like majesty, like god, overtook me. Marcus's hooves kicked up sand, sand immediately swept away by the breeze that came in from the water. His pale chestnut fur was so different from the near-black of my own, and our manes blew wildly. I wasn't sure of his feelings for me at that time, and it may have been influenced by my own feelings toward him, but right then it seemed like we had been taken away into some secret part of the universe that was made just for us. I decided it was called Sandhaven, and I wanted to live in it.

"Marcus, I think I am in love," I shouted, knowing he wouldn't be able to make out my words through the wind.

"Let's run just a little farther," he yelled back. "I know a path we can take back to the village through the woods."

We galloped along like that at a regular pace, feeling the salt-wind on our noses and ears. Then, there was a terrible cracking sound from above and I felt my legs begin to give way, pushing me down, hard into the sand. I noticed that

Marcus had fallen too, and was struggling to get up. The strength I had felt pulsing through my limbs was gone now, replaced by a cold, empty feeling I couldn't place. Where Marcus's gorgeous stallion body had been now was a pile of bleached bones arranged in the shape of a bird.

"Marcus!"de I yelled out.

"What...what are we?" he said, turning his massive, predatory skull toward me.

"I think we're skeletons," I said. "Some large bird of prey."

"Shit."

The sky was black now, and a bright, rose-colored rain had begun to pour down on us. Getting used to the weird, distant sensations of my new body I began to notice a horrible smell. The rain was heavy and acidic, stinging and beating our hollow bones. We wouldn't last long out here.

"Follow me to the woods!" Marcus cried out.

I tried to get to my feet, but between the pain and the darkness I couldn't make sense of my limbs, if they could even be called that. The black of the sky seemed to be pinching through the horizon on either side of us. Some inky mass was getting closer by the second.

I finally got to my feet and awkwardly ran after Marcus, his grotesque form halfway to the woods already, though he was limping heavily. The rain was taking its toll on me as well. Not a hundred yards from the woods I saw Marcus's left leg snap in half, just as I noticed the black seeping toward us from between the trees. The woods weren't safe. Nowhere was safe. I ran over to where Marcus lay, writhing.

"I love you," I said. "I love you I love you I love you I love you I love you I love you."

Marcus turned his head, pink droplets running down his hard beak and through his hollow eye sockets. That was all that I got. A look. He collapsed, his scarred, thin skeleton falling into the sand inaudibly.

"I love you." I whispered it this time, and my body fell down over his.

Sara found herself in a turned house by the sea. The sea was orange and the beach was white and the sky was full of knives. Two men also lived there. In the mornings she would sometimes pretend to be asleep so she could listen to them talk about the sea and the sky-knives. Last night Sara went outside and stared at the moon and felt the salt smell in her nose. She wrote a poem about it:

> *Salt finds salt.*
> *Salt loses salt.*
> *Salt, while driving down the*
> *pennsylvania turnpike in*
> *the late afternoon, smells*
> *a horse-smell, which makes*
> *salt think of salt.*
> *Salt wants desperately to*
> *forget or remember salt.*

The smell made her woozy, and she woke up laying flat on the white beach in front of the orange sea staring straight up into the knives, her inner thighs colored with period blood. Sara felt like she couldn't breathe air anymore. She felt like she needed something else to breathe, some obscure gas like radon or xenon. Her teeth felt angry. She desperately called for the two men but the knives were screaming that time of day and she was sure they wouldn't hear her. She wanted them to come and do something, but she didn't know what. To save her. To pet her hair and feed her ice chips and point out at the orange sea and say beautiful, serious things.

Sara and I met in that place of knives and sea. Neither of us were prepared for war. My skin was sheer and worked like a sieve that my blood kept seeping through. She tried to stop it. I've always been grateful to her for that. It was early morning when the knives were nearly silent, and she was in an awful way. I noticed her hair and the folds in her ears and the blood on her legs I don't think it was mine I don't know for sure there was so much blood. There were two men somewhere away, offstage, and they were always talking about the sea. We were pretending to be asleep, I think, together. Everything was hard to figure out in that place. We had a quiet moment together, me dying and her pushing my blood back in with her hands. In seconds the knives parted and the sky opened up like a split avalanche, like a hurricane stepping aside. I couldn't tell you what happened then except I was crying softly and Sara opened her mouth and aaaaaaaaaaa. I'm sorry I'm not telling this well. What came next was everything.

Nothing disappeared when the knives and sky opened up. What happened was an accident that physics made. Sara was there but so was everything and everything was sorry and everything was tired and everything wanted this just to end already but it wasn't over and it wasn't going to be over. What happens if nothing ever ends? That's the way it is, isn't it? Sara was just sound now just aaaaaaaa and rmmmmm and I don't know. Everything kept making wolf whistles and trying to get a look at her but have you ever looked at sound? I think everything was fucking with you then. I kind of hate everything. Everything unzipped its jeans and made like he was going to I don't know I'm sorry about this this place the men were still talking about the orange sea that was horrible now and then airplanes were over us like hornets but nothing worked out right like I said I think we were under the waves then but I didn't know it was sound or water or did that exist I think I'm repeating myself here. Sara told everything to go go go away she said she didn't want everything she said everything was over and i wanted to cry out that's right but i died then. My sight went and all my blood fell out.

There was a time when I was sitting with Sara on the beach with the turned house and I held her close and looked at her eyes. The knives were humming a whine, a square wave that seemed to be part of it all right then. I wanted to kiss the side of her face and I did. She looked at the orange water like a pack of mad wolves and the knives were still humming and she said there was a boy who lived on a house by the ocean and he used to dive down and find seaweed and he became an expert in seaweed. He knew every kind of seaweed and every use for it. This one plant came to mean so much to him. The knives hummed some more and she kissed me and there was fire.

When Sara was gone, Sara's dog slept 800 days on a beach. He grew his hair out and let the sand and salt mat his fur. He drank salt water and ate rocks. He would look straight out at the clouds near the horizon and push them around with his gaze. All it takes to be a god is to wait until the thing you want happens. It will always happen, eventually, in some way.

Acknowledgements & *thanks*

Pieces from this book were originally published, occasionally in different versions, in the following journals. Deep thanks to these journals and their editors:

UP, Stoked, NAP, Cage Match, Aesthetix, Banango Street, Everyday Genius, Short, Fast & Deadly, Mud Luscious Online, Safety Pin Review, Specter, Dark Sky Magazine, Whole Beast Rag, Menacing Hedge and H_ngm_n.

Sara (the author) would also like to thank the following people for helping this book be a book in their own way: Jeannette Gomes, Jen Tynes, Micheal Sikkema, Chad Redden, Matt Rowan, Carrie Lorig, Aidan Koch, Aral Johnson, Nathan Hoks, Gale Marie Thompson and Dena Rash Guzman.

—⊥—

Sara June Woods is a poet, artist, designer and musician living in Portland, OR. She is the author and designer of two books, *Sara or the Existence of Fire* (which you are holding) and *Wolf Doctors* (Artifice Books, 2014) as well as numerous chapbooks, including *stonepoems* (Solar Luxuriance, 2014) and *rootpoems* (Radioactive Moat, 2013) with Carrie Lorig. Find her online at moonbears.biz.